MOMENTUM

A STEP - BY - STEP SYSTEM FOR GROWING A HEALTHY CHURCH

ERIC SMITH

Published by Eric Smith 2019

All Bible references quoted in this book come from the NIV (New International Version)

Disclaimer
Every effort has been made to ensure that this book is free from error or omissions. Information provided is of general nature only and should not be considered legal or financial advice. The intent is to offer a variety of information to the reader. However, the author, publisher, editor or their agents or representatives shall not accept responsibility for any loss or inconvenience caused to a person or organisation relying on this information.

Book cover design and formatting services by SelfpublishingLab.com

www.momentumswing.net

ISBN
978-1-7336418-0-7 (pbk)
978-1-7336418-1-4 (ebk)

To Krystal, *my amazing wife and best friend:*

You have been my rock since the beginning of my ministry career in college. I am so thankful for your love, encouragement, and sacrifice.

TABLE OF CONTENTS

INTRODUCTION

For the past 17 years I have had the incredible privilege of serving in the church in different capacities. My background before I met Jesus was not in the church. I was living a life that was far from God, but on January 23, 2000, my life was forever changed. I was introduced to a relationship with Jesus, and it was the first time in my life I had experienced peace and fulfillment.

Of course, there have been many days, weeks, and even months since I first became a Jesus follower that I have struggled with fulfillment and joy in my life, but I know that because of Jesus my life now has great purpose. That purpose comes from having a relationship with Jesus that allows me to serve the advancement of the Kingdom of God.

It is following the purpose of God to make an eternal difference that motivates me in my life. I believe the Lord gives all of His followers a purpose that is greater than anything this world can offer. The purpose God gives to His followers is incredibly motivating when it comes to making a difference. When I think about all God has done in my life since I became a Jesus follower, I am motivated and moved to give my best to the work He has called me to.

I think about what Jesus said in John 20:21: "Peace be with you! As the Father has sent me, I am sending you."(NIV) This verse reminds me that just as Jesus was sent with a mission to rescue people, I am also a sent representative of God to share His Good News and make a difference for His Kingdom.

When I think about the weight of eternity, and the people who have yet to meet Jesus, it stirs in me a desire for the church to execute its ministry strategy with precision. I have to be honest and tell you that I have driven myself a little crazy over the years as a student pastor and lead pastor. Over the 17 years of my ministry career, I have always wanted my area of responsibility to be the best it could be for the Lord. This is what has motivated me, and it still drives me to figure out creative ways to help the church be more effective and to operate with precision.

Strategic planning has always been a passion of mine. I have always loved to learn from the leaders inside and outside the church to improve my effectiveness. I understand that some church leaders are hesitant to use ideas from the business world, but often the principles these leaders are using are rooted in biblical teachings. My philosophy has been that if it works and it is not in opposition to the scriptures, then use it.

I did not grow up in the church, so I have to confess that there is not a traditional bone in my body. I have never been motivated to do things just because they have always been done in a certain way. As church leaders, we must accept the reality that the church in North America is declining.

I am convinced that one of the reasons we are losing people and struggling to reach new people is operational deficiency. According to David Olson in his book, *The American Church in Crisis*, the percentage of Americans who attend a Christian church on any given weekend has declined from 20.4 percent in 1990 to 17.5 percent in 2005.

Over the last ten years as a senior pastor I have spent a great deal of time working on how to operate more effectively in the churches I have led. I have always lived with the belief that if someone gives us the honor and privilege of coming to our church, we should honor them by serving them well in every possible way.

I have always wanted our team to have a strategic plan and to make sure that nothing falls through the cracks. Over the years, my teams and I have used multiple tools and strategies and learned a lot through multiple successes and failures. The process of trial and error has led to the writing of this book. The Momentum model is designed specifically to improve the operation of churches and other organizations to impact the world for Christ.

Momentum is a step-by-step operating system for churches and other organizations that will help them become more effective and efficient. My prayer is that God will use it to help the churches and other organizations grow and become healthier for God's Kingdom. My ultimate passion and desire is to see more people become Jesus followers. As a Jesus follower myself, I want my decisions and leadership to align with His word. Over the years of being a Jesus follower, I have studied many different examples of leadership and strategy in the Bible. In this book you will see a few of those examples, with the first being from the life of Moses.

A biblical basis for strategy

Moses was a strategic thinker. In the scripture we learn that he grew as a strategic thinker. He faced challenges as a leader after he had led the nation of Israel out of Egypt. Jethro, his father-in-law, came to see him after hearing the incredible things God had been doing. Moses was overwhelmed, so Jethro shared with him a God-given principle for dealing with the challenges he faced. From Exodus 18:9–26:

- "Jethro was delighted to hear about all the good things the Lord had done for Israel in rescuing them from the hand of the Egyptians." (verse 9)
- "He said, 'Praise be to the Lord, who rescued you from the hand of the Egyptians and of Pharaoh, and who rescued the people from the hand of the Egyptians.'" (verse 10)
- "Now I know that the Lord is greater than all other gods, for he did this to those who had treated Israel arrogantly." (verse 11)
- "Then Jethro, Moses' father-in-law, brought a burnt offering and other sacrifices to God, and Aaron came with all the elders of Israel to eat a meal with Moses' father-in-law in the presence of God." (verse 12)

- "The next day Moses took his seat to serve as judge for the people, and they stood around him from morning till evening." (verse 13)
- "When his father-in-law saw all that Moses was doing for the people, he said, 'What is this you are doing for the people? Why do you alone sit as judge, while all these people stand around you from morning till evening?'" (verse 14)
- "Moses answered him, 'Because the people come to me to seek God's will.'" (verse 15)
- "Whenever they have a dispute, it is brought to me, and I decide between the parties and inform them of God's decrees and instructions." (verse 16)
- "Moses' father-in-law replied, 'What you are doing is not good.'" (verse 17)
- "You and these people who come to you will only wear yourselves out. The work is too heavy for you; you cannot handle it alone." (verse 18)
- "Listen now to me and I will give you some advice, and may God be with you. You must be the people's representative before God and bring their disputes to him." (verse19)
- "Teach them his decrees and instructions, and show them the way they are to live and how they are to behave." (verse 20)

- "But select capable men from all the people—men who fear God, trustworthy men who hate dishonest gain—and appoint them as officials over thousands, hundreds, fifties and tens." (verse 21)
- "Have them serve as judges for the people at all times, but have them bring every difficult case to you; the simple cases they can decide themselves. That will make your load lighter, because they will share it with you." (verse 22)
- "If you do this and God so commands, you will be able to stand the strain, and all these people will go home satisfied." (veres 23)
- "Moses listened to his father-in-law and did everything he said." (verse 24)
- "He chose capable men from all Israel and made them leaders of the people, officials over thousands, hundreds, fifties and tens." (verse 25)
- "They served as judges for the people at all times. The difficult cases they brought to Moses, but the simple ones they decided themselves." (verse 26)

Jethro coached Moses on setting up a strategy for delegating the work so the load would be spread among many. As a result of this strategic plan, more people were engaged and empowered with responsibility. The resources were used more effectively and the work was accomplished more efficiently. Moses learned from this experience with Jethro and continued to act strategically.

Another great example of Moses leading strategically is when he sent spies to the land of Canaan in the Old Testament Book of Numbers, chapter 13.

These are just two of many biblical examples that teach us the importance of having a strategy. The Book of Proverbs gives multiple verses that teach us the importance of being strategic and intentional. Here are three more on the subject of planning and strategizing with others:

- "The plans of the diligent lead surely to abundance, but everyone who is hasty comes only to poverty." (Proverbs 21:5)
- "Plans fail for lack of counsel, but with many advisers they succeed." (Proverbs 15:22)
- "Commit to the Lord whatever you do, and your plans will succeed." (Proverbs 16:3)

Jesus was also very strategic during his earthly ministry. He gave his disciples a strategy for spreading the Gospel in Acts 1:8. In the following verse, Jesus gives us the blueprint strategy for missions relating to the church: "But you will receive power when the Holy

Spirit has come on you, and you will be my witnesses in Jerusalem, in all Judea and Samaria, and to the end of the earth." (Acts 1:8)

Jesus gave the disciples four areas in which to spread His message: Jerusalem, Judea, Samaria, and to the end of the earth. This strategy was specific to the disciples he was sending out as His representatives at that time in history, but it can also be a blueprint for our strategic-missions strategy in the church today.

Jerusalem was home base for the disciples. The second area Jesus sent the disciples to was Judea, the region where they lived. The third area Jesus mentioned was Samaria. This area was looked down upon by the disciples, who saw the Samaritan people as half-breeds. The racial tension and animosity between the two groups was very high. The last area Jesus sent His disciples to was the end of the earth. This was a call to take the message of His Good News to people who had never heard it. This was a call to go with the Gospel message of hope to all people.

The point here is this, God is strategic, as His people, we should also be strategic so we can be most effective in what we are attempting to accomplish. This is a blueprint for the church to apply today and ask: Where is our Jerusalem, Judea, Samaria, and end of the earth?

The nuts and bolts

Anyone who has worked in a church or any other organization, you know there is always room for growth and improvement. The Momentum model has been created to help leaders lead more effectively. Momentum is a step-by-step operating system that can be implemented in any church. It was born out of a desire to improve the operation of the churches I have served, but it has become a process that can be helpful to all leaders who are willing to implement the system and tools. The style or denomination of the church doesn't matter because the process is designed to work within most organizational structures. It is important to mention that for momentum to work it is essential for the leader of the church to have the authority to make decisions. It is also important for the leader of the church to be a learner and willing to listen to the team. If the leader is a learner and a team player, then momentum has the potential to help drastically.

The reality is that every church has an operating system, the important question for us here is: does it work? As a leader, ask yourself this question about your own church: Is our current system producing the results we desire?

As a leader, you must understand that every church has a culture, and that culture is shaped by the way things are done and the way values are lived out. Our desire is to help you, as a leader, be intentional about the culture you create by implementing the Momentum model and tools to grow your desired culture. Momentum will help you clarify your vision, build relational trust, and grow a healthy culture.

CHAPTER 1

The Momentum System

In this chapter I will give a broad overview of the Momentum system and how it works. Momentum has five key elements, and each element has within it specific tools that will help you. As a leader, I'm sure you desire to see your church become healthier and grow numerically. For this to happen, however, the necessary changes that must be made can be difficult and can also take time. It won't happen overnight or even in six months. This book is written for you to use the system and implement the tools, but for many leaders they would invite coaching and training to do implementation.

For one of our certified Momentum trainers to serve your organization in implement the overall process, it is an 18-month journey. We believe however that the results are worth the work. If Momentum is something you and your team want to implement, our recommendation is to work with one of our Momentum trainers to help you on your journey. Of course, you can choose to self-implement, but implementation with a certified Momentum trainer will increase the odds of success.

The five key elements of Momentum

Momentum has five key elements. The following is a brief description of each element, plus the tools that make up each.

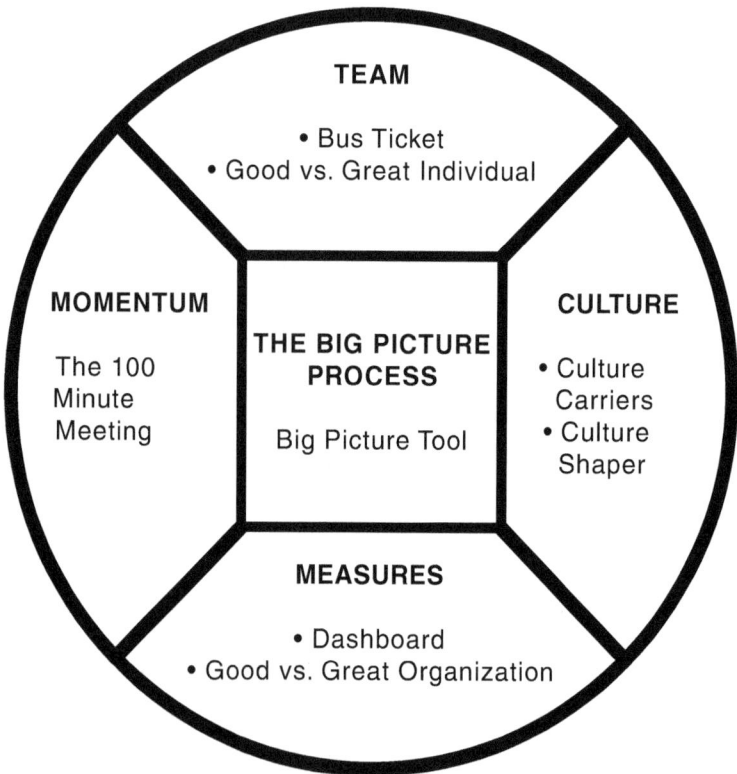

TEAM
- Bus Ticket
- Good vs. Great Individual

MOMENTUM

The 100 Minute Meeting

THE BIG PICTURE PROCESS

Big Picture Tool

CULTURE
- Culture Carriers
- Culture Shaper

MEASURES
- Dashboard
- Good vs. Great Organization

Element #1 Big-Picture Process

This element helps to get your whole leadership team on the same page and moving in the same direction:

- Big-picture tool: This tool brings clarity around the organization's purpose statement, core values, overall direction, and future vision. This tool has ten questions that the leadership team answers and revisits every three months to make sure they are staying on track.

Element #2 Team

This element has two tools that have been designed to help your team members understand expectations and manage their time better:

- Bus-ticket tool: This tool helps leaders determine if the right people are on the bus, and if they are in the right seats on the bus.
- Good-vs.-great-individual tool: This tool helps each team member evaluate and maximize the benefits of their schedule and responsibilities. This tool

will help to strengthen the contribution of all team members and make them more effective and efficient in their designed roles.

Element #3 Culture

This element helps shape the desired culture in alignment with the core values you want on your leadership team and the culture you want within your church body as a whole. The two tools within this element will help you achieve your desired culture:

- Culture-carrier tool: This tool is designed to strategically build "culture carriers" on your leadership team through relational trust, understanding, and cultural alignment.
- Culture-shaper tool: This tool is designed to develop a multisensory strategy and delivery system to communicate the church's core values in memorable and innovative ways.

Element #4 Measures

This element is used to help the church determine what is great over what is good as well as what is actually important in measuring success.

- Dashboard tool: This tool will assist your team in determining what numbers are important for you to track. This needs to be in alignment with your values and vision. In other words, it is more than simply counting people and money.
- Good-vs.-great-organization tool: Ideally, your staff team will use this tool to filter the church calendar and their ministry calendar. This should reveal what needs to be delegated, focused on, or even stopped.

Element #5 Momentum

The fifth element is Momentum. It includes the 100-minute-meeting-tool to keep everything moving forward:

- 100-minute-meeting tool: This tool is the key to making each week effective. It helps the team execute the first element, Big-Picture Process, which should be reviewed every three months. The 100-minute-meeting tool creates accountability and builds in a system for things to be accomplished.

As you and your team begin this journey, we invite you to take our organizational culture audit. It is very important that your whole team take this audit to evaluate the current state of your culture. (If you would prefer to do this online, there is a digital version of this audit on the Momentum website: www.momentumswing.net.)

Organizational culture audit

Score each of the following questions from 1–5. It is extremely important that you answer honestly. Do not answer based on the way you wish things were, but instead on how you perceive things to be. It is important for this to be a confidential test so the person taking it can be honest. The audit evaluates five areas: trust, accountability, commitment, personal value, and communication. To determine your overall score, add up the individual scores from these combinations of questions:

Strongly agree	Agree	Neutral	Disagree	Strongly disagree
5	4	3	2	1

1. There is a high level of trust within the staff team. _____

2. There is a high level of expectation that everyone will do their job with excellence. _____

3. The people I work with are dedicated to fulfilling our church's vision. _____

4. I feel cared for on this team. _____

5. I can ask hard and honest questions of my supervisor. _____

6. The majority of our church members trust the ministry staff team. _____

7. The expectations are clear for what my supervisor expects of me. _____

8. I believe the staff members are living out the church's purpose statement. _____

9. I love being on this team and serving in my position. _____

10. My ideas are heard and considered by my team members. _____

11. The staff team members are dedicated to achieving the goals set by the senior leaders. _____

12. The staff team members are held accountable when fulfilling their responsibilities. _____

13. I believe in the direction our church is going. _____

14. I receive helpful feedback from my supervisor. _____

15. Our staff team is effectively communicating the vision and values of the church to our volunteer teams.

_____

16. My supervisor trusts me to lead and manage my responsibilities. _____

17. Staff members are held accountable when they fail to accomplish their responsibilities. _____

18. I believe the core values are being lived by the majority of our church members. _____

19. We have a healthy work-and-life balance as church staff members. _____

20. Our volunteers clearly understand the church's core values. _____

	Score
Trust: Add the scores from questions 1, 6, 11, 16	
Accountability: Add the scores from questions 2, 7, 12, 17	
Commitment: Add the scores from questions 3, 8, 13, 18	

	Score
Personal value: Add the scores from questions 4, 9, 14, 19	
Communication: Add the scores from questions 5, 10, 15, 20	
Total score	

Whatever your organizations score, use it as a gauge to determine the areas that need work. Every organization has room to grow, so use the culture audit learn how you and your team can go to the next level of healthy and effective leadership.

The organizational culture audit evaluates five specific areas:

1. Trust
2. Accountability
3. Commitment
4. Personal value
5. Communication

We consider a score of 16–20 as healthy, with 20 being the healthiest. This allows you to identify specific areas that need attention. Your overall score might be 80 or above overall, but there still might be an area that needs attention. If your overall score is below 80, then identify the areas for growth and work on improving those areas with the Momentum tools.

In the following chapters I will share some practical stories of real challenges leaders face in leading churches. The stories will show how each Momentum element and its accompanying tools can help improve your church.

⬈ RECAP

Hopefully you now have a broad understanding of the five elements that make up Momentum and the tools that each element uses to make up the overall Momentum model. I recommend that you come back to this chapter, when needed, as a reference as you work through each subsequent chapter. Something very important to understand is that you do not implement each of the tools at the same time. The Big Picture tool and the 100-minute meeting tool are the first tools you implement and they are used weekly. The other tools are implemented over the first year of following the Momentum model. When you bring your team together to go through the Big Picture tool every three months teach them 1 or 2 of the other 6 tools until all 6 tools are being used. By first year you and your team will understand each of the tools and be using them to improve the effectiveness of the organization.

I also recommend that a year after you have been operating with the Momentum model, your team takes the organizational culture audit again and then compares the results to the first time.

In the next chapter we take an in-depth look at the Big-Picture Process and the Big-Picture tool. This element can give you and your team the clarity and unity you have desired.

CHAPTER 2

Big-Picture Process

Pastor John founded Community Church and had been pastoring the church for six years. There had been so much excitement and energy at the start of the new church. The team was dedicated to the success of this new church, and they invited all their friends and family to the grand-opening service. After a year of praying, planning, and working to launch Community Church, the dream had become a reality. The grand-opening service was a huge success, with 200 people in attendance. Their goal as a launch team was to see 150 people; they exceeded their goal and were off and running.

The next two years were a whirlwind of ups and downs in the church. As with any new church, some of the early adopters were now gone. This was hard on Pastor John because he felt as though people had quit on him and the church.

The financial challenges of a new church were also a struggle over the first two years because although the numbers were growing fast, many of the people who were part of the church didn't have the discipline of giving. This made things challenging financially, but the church's needs were met and it was able to keep growing.

The church that had started with 200 people at the grand opening now had an attendance of 400 people. The church was starting to run out of space in the school where they met on Sundays. This led the team to start working to find a new location.

After three months of praying and searching, the church leaders decided to construct their own building. They believed that if they could get a new building it would help see them through their next wave of numerical growth. It took a year to construct the new building but finally it was time to move in.

The church had seen a decline of 50 people who were against the new building. This was disappointing, because by now the church was averaging 350 people on a typical Sunday, and giving was down slightly from the year before.

They finally opened the new church at the beginning of their fourth year, and the excitement sparked growth over the next months. There were 75 new people in weekly attendance and now they were back to 425 people each Sunday.

The two years that followed after moving into the new building were challenging. The church had been numerically stagnant for two years, and the only new growth they had seen was when they first moved into their new building. The majority of the new people would tell Pastor John when they saw him, "We love the new building. We'd been waiting for you to become a real church and get a building, so now that you are, we come here."

This really bothered Pastor John, because he felt that many of the new people were not there because of the church's vision or to help them grow, but just for themselves.

The stress of constructing the new building, plus staff issues, overextended Pastor John. The staff and Pastor John started to feel like they were just going through the motions. They had lost their long-range vision; the staff team seemed to be working hard, but none of them really knew the plan. The team was stuck, and Pastor John felt like he and the church were hitting a wall.

The burnout that Pastor John was feeling created a mental block, and he was unable to see the future God had for their church. He didn't know what to do to rediscover the vision and strategy they had had when they first began.

Pastor John knew that he and his team needed some help to break through the wall. He kept making excuses, for instance, that they didn't have the money to hire someone to help them. He battled personal pride in having someone else step in to assist them. He also convinced himself that he was too busy to take the time to get outside help.

Finally Pastor John decided to call a trusted pastor friend he had served with for several years before starting Community Church. His pastor friend told John that he believed getting some outside help would be extremely beneficial, and Pastor John agreed. After Pastor John got off the phone, however, he began to make all the excuses in his mind again as to why he couldn't do it, or didn't need the help. Pastor John had some big decisions to make about the future of his church.

Big-picture tool

The story of Pastor John and Community Church is a very common one, and one that many churches face. Leading any organization is filled with challenges and barriers that keep leaders from going to the next level. They often get stuck and cannot seem to find a way to gain traction in their organization. The challenges they face can cloud their leadership, making it hard for them to see the future.

The Big-Picture Process element has a simple tool called the big-picture tool. The goal is to take a leader and their leadership team through ten questions to help the team step outside of the church and get clarity. After the team uses the big-picture tool to do this, they repeat the process every three months to drill down and make sure everyone is on the same page. The repetition also helps the team make any changes to the answers they have given to the ten questions. The ten questions that make up this tool will help the team be unified around where they plan to go.

If the staff team doesn't know where the leader is going, they will have a hard time following. Using this tool will help the leader really *hear* what their team thinks and will also force the leader to put that down on paper. This process will help the team accomplish more and go further.

As mentioned, the big-picture-tool process should be repeated every three months as long as you choose to use the Momentum model. If you hire one of our certified Momentum trainers, they will work with you for at least eighteen months to implement the process. After the eighteen months, we encourage you to continue using the big-picture tool every three months.

You will use the tool to set your agenda for your church for the next three months, and indefinitely. The ten questions that make up the big-picture tool:

1. What is your purpose statement?

This is a question that most leaders have heard, and you may already have a purpose statement. If you do not have one, then it is important to define what is the ultimate purpose: the reason why your church exists. One important thing I always encourage when crafting a purpose statement is to make it as short and concise as possible. Often we try to say too much; keep your purpose statement focused and simple.

We advise you to have a whiteboard session as you answer the ten questions. The goal is to have a clear purpose statement that everyone knows and can remember.

Think of the purpose statement as a lighthouse that always guides your *why* as an organization. It is important that anyone who is on your leadership team is fully committed to achieving the organization's purpose. Never assume that people know the purpose. Make sure to continually to repeat the purpose and celebrate when it's being fulfilled.

Every three months, use the big-picture tool to set your next three-month agenda at the senior-level team meeting. The senior-level team can be whoever you as the leader determine needs to be part of guiding your organization through the Momentum. The first thing you will do each time is go back over your purpose statement.

2. What are your core values?

The core values of any organization are the core beliefs and behaviors. The tension that always exists in determining core values comes from trying to determine what will be listed and what will be left off the list. I recommend that you make several hard choices and determine what will be your top four or five core values. I am a big believer that less is more when it comes to core values. The reason I encourage fewer core values is because, as you work through the momentum model, your core values will be essential in growing and shaping the culture of the organization. A long list of core values will make the process more difficult.

After you list the four to five core values of your organization, I encourage you to take the core values and make "sticky statements" these are very short statements that are memorable and can be easily repeated. Sticky statements allow the people in your organization to communicate core values more easily and effectively. The process of determining these core values and sticky statements is best accomplished with a team of people working together.

Every three months, revisit the big-picture tool to set your next three-month agenda at the senior-level team meeting. Part of that process will be going back through your core values again.

3. What is your five-year dream?

The practice of writing down the five-year dream and vision for where you see God taking the church is a key step in setting a direction for the team to work toward. This will help the senior leadership get on the same page and pass along that long-range vision to the rest of their team and the people involved in their areas of responsibility.

Some leaders like to determine a ten- or twenty-year dream, and that is fine. I believe, however, that culture and situations are changing faster than ever before, so it can be difficult to project further than five years. The people on the team will probably have an easier time seeing five years than ten or twenty.

Every three months, revisit your five-year dream at your senior-level team meeting.

4. What is unique about your church?

Whoa? lw?

Each church has unique things to offer its community. It is important to identify and leverage your own uniques that exist for growth. Uniques are those things that, I believe, God gives you to leverage for the effectiveness of your organization or church.

You senior-leadership team should have a discussion to determine what your uniques are, and even ask people who have come to be part of the organization or church why they came. Feedback from those in the congregation can often reveal the reasons why they came, and that will help you identify the uniques that your organization possesses. A couple examples of uniques would be a dynamic kids ministry or racial diversity, etc.

Every three months, revisit your uniques at the senior-level team meeting.

Local

Next gen ministry — Community Outreach

5. Who is your target group to reach?

It is important to determine your primary target group. This process will help you know how to best market your church to the audience you believe you are called to reach. It will also impact how you design your graphics, how you communicate on social media, and the style of worship that you offer. The style of preaching and communication is based on your target group. I believe that having a focused target group will make you and your team more effective at reaching more people.

As you are determining who your target group is, study who lives in the area you minister. Also, look culturally at the lifestyle and mindset of those who live around your church: their values, interests, hurts, and fears. Lastly, who do you believe you are called to reach as a church?

Every three months, revisit the target group at the senior-level team meeting.

6. What is your three-year dream?

The three-year dream can seem repetitive because you have already listed your five-year dream, but it's important because it makes you think about the steps to take over the next three years to accomplish your five-year dream. As you look back over your five-year dream, think about what you want to accomplish in the next three years that could lead you closer to your five-year dream. This is an important conversation because it will set the pace for the team and draw the long-range goals closer.

Every three months, revisit your three-year dream at the senior-level team meeting.

7. What is your one-year dream?

After the team has come up with your three-year dream, determine what you dream to accomplish during the next year. This is very important because it will determine your focus. This list of goals should be SMART (specific, measurable, actionable, relevant, and time-bound). It can take a lot of mental focus to think about this over the coming year, and then to look beyond that to three years, and five years. I believe this process is essential to accomplishing your long-range dreams.

Every three months, revisit your one-year goals at the senior level-team meeting.

8. What are your ITAs for the next three months?

Your ITAs (items to accomplish) are those things that your organization needs to accomplish over the next three months. ITAs are determined by what the team and senior leadership decided were the five-year, three-year, and one-year dreams. In order to accomplish your one-year dream, what do you need to accomplish over the next three months?

As with the one-year dream, this list of goals should also be SMART (specific, measurable, actionable, relevant, and time-bound). It can take some mental focus to think over long-range goals and determine what needs to be accomplished to achieving them.

Every three months, set new ITAs for the organization as a whole. Also, each leader for each department should also set a list of ITAs for themselves and the area they are responsible for. This is a critical list of things that must be accomplished before each and every three-month senior-level team meeting.

The list of ITAs should consist of 4 to 6 of the most important things you want to accomplish for each team member, and 4 to 6 of the most important things for the organization. Some of these might be on both the organization's list and individuals' lists. This creates a three-month window for the team to operate in, and will create focus and synergy to get more things done on a consistent basis.

Think of it this way: a football team on the offensive side is trying to get the ball in the end zone for a touchdown. In my mind, I see the five-year dream as the end zone, and every step in the big-picture tool is a potential play in the offensive series to get the ball where it should be. You and your team have to drive the ball down the field. The big-picture tool is the offensive for you and your team to methodically move the ball down the field to score.

9. What current obstacles exist?

Every church faces obstacles that stand in the way of their dreams. As a team, it is extremely helpful to identify these obstacles that prevent you from realizing your vision and then to create a plan to remove them. The obstacles might be internal or external. The main thing is to be honest. Once you identify the obstacles, you can come up with a way to remove them. A couple examples of obstacles could be disunity on your team, facility quality, or people who are unwilling to change. The list of obstacles can be unique to each situation.

29

Every three months, revisit your obstacle list at the senior-level team meeting because new ones will typically arise.

10. Are there any organizational blindspots?

The conversation to determine organizational blindspots can be uncomfortable, but it is essential. Often the blindspot is unseen by the leaders however a blindspot is a blindspot. It can be helpful to have a Momentum trainer or trusted mentor help your team identify potential blindspots. Many times identifying blindspots is the difference between success and failure when you take a risk or try to implement a new strategy.

Every three months, revisit your blindspot list at the senior-level team meeting because a new one might have been identified.

Big Picture Process

Page 1

Purpose Statement	Core Values
	1.
	2.
	3.
	4.
	5.
5-Year Dream	3-5 Uniques
1.	1.
2.	2.
3.	3.
4.	4.
5.	5.
Current Obstacles	

31

Big Picture Process

Target Group	3-Year Dream
	1.
	2.
	3.
	4.
	5.
1-Year Goals	**ITA (Items to Accomplish)**
	1.
2.	2.
3.	3.
4.	4.
5.	5.
Blind Spots	

↗RECAP

As a leader, you have probably asked the ten questions that make up the big-picture tool at some point on your leadership journey. The strength of using the tool is in finding out the answers to these questions, and then every three months coming back to them and asking them all over again. This should become part of your ongoing meeting culture. This will keep your team focused on your purpose, core values, and long-range plans. The big-picture process can be a game-changer for your organization.

In the next chapter we take a look at the second element of Momentum called Team. This element of the process gives two practice tools to help your team be more effective.

CHAPTER 3

Team

Pastor Tim and his family moved to Arizona after he had served at a church in Texas for several years as a pastor. He took the senior-pastor position at First Church in Tucson. The church had been on a slight numerical decline for the previous decade, but they were in a growing area of the city and Pastor Tim believed that with God's help they could turn things around.

Over the next three years the church saw attendance increase each Sunday from an average of 325 to 450 people. The church had a buzz from all the growth, and the excitement was evident. The church had not seen growth in many years.

As the church grew and became financially stronger, it became time for Pastor Tim to hire two more pastors to join his team. He already had a family pastor and a worship pastor, but he wanted to add a discipleship pastor and a kids' pastor. He began the interview process focusing on who had the most experience and the most education. He made the two hires and was excited about the two new pastors joining the First Church staff team.

The first six months were a great honeymoon time, with the two new pastors and the existing team having a great time working together and getting to know each other. Then Pastor Tim thought it would be a great idea to have a staff retreat. The team would go away for three days to discuss the future and plan for the upcoming year.

On the first day of the retreat, Pastor Tim began to share his vision for the future of the church, the changes he wanted to make in the upcoming years, and the church's core values. At dinner that night the new discipleship pastor started questioning Pastor Tim about one of the values he had mentioned. The core value in question, as stated by Pastor Tim, was: "We must take radical risks to reach the lost."

The new discipleship pastor began to ask questions about reaching the lost, including the risks involved in doing so, and it became clear that the new pastor was not willing to take the radical risks that Pastor Tim was. As the conversation unfolded, the new pastor told Pastor Tim that if they would just "preach the Word of God" then they would reach those that God intended for them to reach.

Pastor Tim agreed that the Word of God needed to be preached, but the church also had to be willing to do radical things to reach people that no one else was reaching. The dinner ended awkwardly and the team members went to their rooms for the night.

The next day, when they began their morning session, the new kids' pastor brought up the conversation from the night before and agreed with Pastor Tim that radical risks had to be taken to reach the lost. The worship pastor, who had been on staff at the church prior to Pastor Tim, spoke up and agreed with the new discipleship pastor.

After this dialogue, Pastor Tim realized that the team was divided. He knew that honest debate and disagreement was healthy, but the team members clearly had different values, and he knew that the culture would remain fractured because of the divide. He was torn on what to do. Should he try to convince the worship pastor and discipleship pastor to change their views, or should he help them move on and find new jobs?

This story of Pastor Tim and his team is not unusual. There are church staff teams that are extremely divided, and this can act like a cancer that erodes the team's trust. As leaders, we want our teams to be united around a common vision and the values of our organizations, because that determines whether the culture will be healthy and contagious. If a leadership is divided, it can be very difficult to gain traction. I know that in my own leadership positions I have faced division among team members regarding vision and values. In those situations it is very difficult to be effective.

The second key element of Momentum is Team. This element is devoted to helping you hire and develop the right people to be on your bus. You can also use it to help you determine who to fire, if necessary.

The tool that you will use to accomplish these tasks is called the bus-ticket tool, which is designed to help you take your vision and your values and ask the right questions to determine who should be on your team. There is also a section of the tool that helps you determine if people are in the right seats on the bus. This is not a tool to condemn people, but instead to empower and align them. "Therefore encourage one another and build each other up as you are already doing." (I Thessalonians 5:11)

Bus-ticket tool

The bus-ticket tool is about encouragement and building others up. It is a tool that helps open the lines of communication within the staff team for authentic instruction and direction. We all get better when we are aligned around a common vision and values.

Bus Ticket Tool

Answer (Yes, Maybe, or No)

		Name		
	Vision			
	Value #1			
The Right Bus	Value #2			
	Value #3			
	Value #4			
	Value #5			
	Get it			
The Right Seat	Ability			
	Passion			

The top section of the tool is focused on whether the person should be on the bus, and the bottom section is focused on the seat they should sit in on the bus. To use this tool, write down the name of the person you are evaluating at the top of the table. Then list your values down the side under value #1, value #2, etc. Then have the team score the team member with a *yes*, *maybe*, or *no*. Repeat the process at the bottom of the tool, which evaluates whether the person is in the right seat on the bus. This is also scored with a *yes*, *maybe*, or *no*.

Following are the next steps your team can take, depending on the answer you give to each person and the area you are evaluating.

- If the person gets a *yes*, celebrate their alignment and effectiveness.

    Next steps for being on the bus: Celebrate their alignment as a team member and personally thank them. Remember that what is rewarded is repeated.

    Next steps for being in the right seat on the bus: Encourage them in the job they are doing. Remember that what is rewarded is repeated.

- If the person gets a *maybe*, have a conversation about why and how to resolve the issue.

    Next steps for being on the bus: Create a 60-day action plan to help them move from a *maybe* to a *yes* in the value list. Ask them to write out why they align with and believe each of the church's values.

Next steps for being in the right seat on the bus: If the *maybe* is in the GAP (Get it, Ability to do the job, Passion for the job) area, have them work during the 60-day period toward showing you why they should be in that particular seat on the bus.

- If the person gets a *no,* communicate your concern about why they don't align with the church's values and might need to be removed from the team. If they get a *no* in the GAP area, they might need to be moved to a different seat on the bus.

Next steps for being on the bus: If the person gets a *no* on a value alignment, the first step is to meet with them and discuss the church's values to make sure there is no misunderstanding. If they indicate an issue with one of the values and are unable to get on board, action needs to be taken to remove them from the team.

Next steps for being in the right seat on the bus: If the person gets a *no* in the GAP area, have a discussion with your leadership team to see if there is another seat that would better fit that person. If there is another seat, then meet with the person and encourage them to make the move to a better seat on the bus.

Good-vs.-great-individual tool

This tool was created to help staff members better manage their time and responsibilities. In the book of Ephesians we learn to make the most of our time. To not waste the time we have been given on less important things when we can do great and important things: "Look carefully then how you walk, not as unwise but as wise, making the best use of the time, because the days are evil. Therefore do not be foolish, but understand what the will of the Lord is." (Ephesians 5:15–17)

The goal of this tool is take your calendar and responsibilities and remove the bad, delegate some of the good, and focus on the great. This tool can help staff members focus their time and energy on activities that produce the best results, and align with the organization's goals.

There are two versions of this tool, but they are used in the same way. The individual version, which is the one used in the Team element of the Momentum process, is for an individual team member to list their ongoing responsibilities and calendar items in one of the four quadrants.

1. Top-right quadrant: high impact/high return = great results
2. Top-left quadrant: high impact/low return = good results
3. Bottom-right quadrant: low impact/high return = good results
4. Bottom-left quadrant: low impact/low return = bad results

When you have made this evaluation, you are ready to move onto the next step:

- Bad results: Items that fall in the bottom-left quadrant should be placed on a list to be stopped immediately, or a plan needs to be put in place to remove the items from the person's calendar or responsibilities.
- Good results: Items that fall in the top-left or bottom-right quadrant need to be reviewed, and the individual needs to determine how to delegate or give less of their time to the less productive items.
- Great results: Items that fall in the top-right quadrant indicate a need for the individual to give them more time and attention. These are the items that give the greatest results and have the greatest impact

and return. It is important to make this more of the individual's focus.

Individual

Good vs. Great Tool

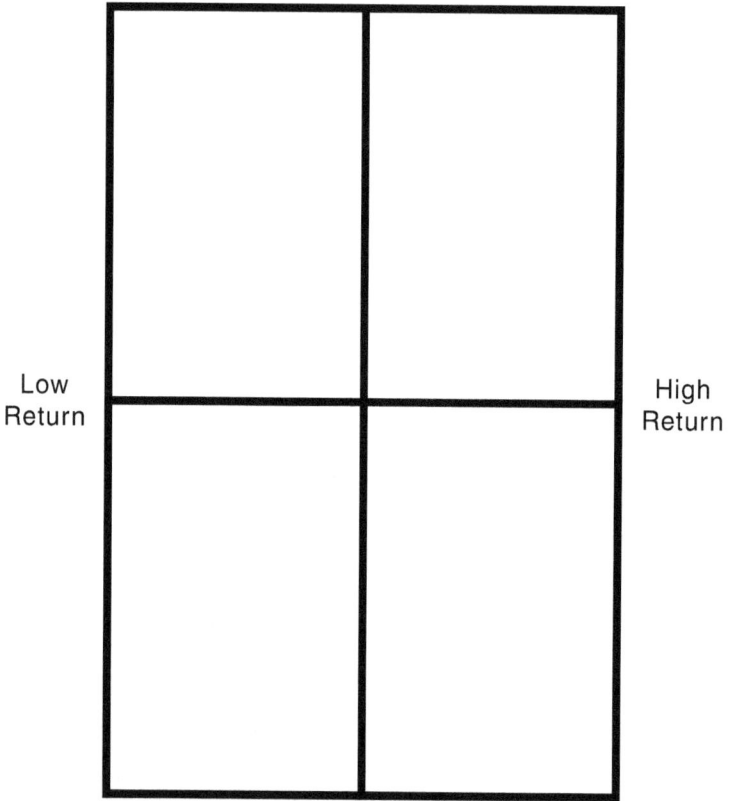

High Impact

Low
Return

High
Return

Low Impact

↗RECAP

If there is one thing I have learned the hard way, it is that an organization's team is everything. It is the team members who make an organization effective. That might be team members who are paid, or those who are on the team as volunteers, but there is no doubt that having the right people makes the difference to being great or merely being average. My hope is that you will become well versed in using the bus-ticket tool to evaluate your current team members and also to craft questions as you are interviewing potential team members.

Also, learn to use the good-vs.-great-individual tool to help your team manage their time and focus on what matters most. This is why having the big-picture tool is so important: by using it you will have defined what matters most to you, and that will help your team use the good-vs.-great-individual tool to know what to devote their time to.

In the next chapter we will work through Culture, the next element in the Momentum model.

CHAPTER 4

Culture

The third key element of Momentum is Culture. The right culture is critical if you are going to have a healthy long-term impact as an organization. As a leader, I have failed multiple times and developed cultures that were not very healthy. I have also succeeded and developed cultures that *were* healthy.

When a leader has experienced both unhealthy and healthy cultures, they can easily tell the difference. Of course, for a culture to be healthy it needs to have healthy people who are united together. (This is why the second element of the Momentum process is Team. The Team element comes before Culture to strive to get the right people on the bus and in the right seats.)

I have had the privilege of being part of pastoring two fast-growing churches. One of the churches we planted, and the other one we helped revitalize. The one we helped revitalize was an incredible learning experience. When we arrived there, I had never seen a more toxic culture. It was a shock to see how divisive and mean some of the church members were. It was because of that experience that I now understand why some people leave the church and never come back.

Some of the meanest people on Earth are in churches across America, and they are tearing churches apart and destroying the lives of pastors and church leaders.

I knew that we needed to have a drastic shift in the culture of the church we revitalized, so from day one I focused on building trust with key leaders by spending time with them. The other thing I did was to make every decision through the lens of what I judged to be the healthiest thing to do. It was painful the first year because we lost a lot of the people who were divisive, but we had to remove the cancer of divisiveness to get to a place where we could become healthy.

As a staff team, and as lay leadership teams, we focused on our values. We put plans in place to live out our values together, and a plan to communicate them in innovative ways to bring the typical church member and newcomer on board.

It was amazing to see what God did when we made hard choices in deciding what was healthy and aligned with the core values. We saw the church become a life-giving culture, and we experienced incredible numerical and spiritual growth. The hard choice of removing the negativity and replacing it with positivity led us to become one of the fastest-growing churches in America. During the unhealthy season, the church had solid preaching, music, family ministries, but the culture was toxic. I believe that when a culture is toxic it will eventually erode the foundation.

When the culture became healthier the church started thriving. A healthy culture is shaped by a united group of people living out a set of core values, all moving in the same direction for a common purpose. This is what we experienced eventually, but it took hard work, painful decisions, and intentionality. The book of Titus and Romans teaches us how to handle divisive people: "As for a person who stirs up division, after warning him once and then twice, have nothing more to do with him." (Titus 3:10) "I appeal to you, brothers, to watch out for those who cause divisions and create obstacles contrary to the doctrine that you have been taught; avoid them." (Romans 16:17)

Professor Richard Perrin said: "Organizational culture is the sum of values and rituals which serve as 'glue' to integrate the members of the organization." Other leaders have said that culture is "the way we do things here." Our desire is to help organizations improve their culture by intentionally living out their values as a team. It is also to help them communicate their values to the people they are trying to engage. Organizations will often have a great product but a toxic, or unclear, culture. The same is true of churches: they can have great preaching and music, but if the culture is unhealthy the foundation will eventually erode.

The culture of an organization can make or break your long-term effectiveness. If the culture is healthy, focused on its purpose, and is life giving, people will want to join the movement. If the culture is dysfunctional, toxic, and draining, people will run away as fast as possible. I believe people are longing for things that add value and give them life. If your church has a toxic culture it could be very difficult to overcome.

Pastor Chris Hodges of Church of the Highlands says: "Culture trumps vision." I agree with Chris because I have seen this firsthand. If the culture is toxic and unhealthy, the vision will get stuck and in many cases fall apart. Also, Peter Drucker says "culture eats strategy for breakfast". The lesson for leaders is the culture of your organization is essential for the success of your organization. The culture must be worked on, intentionally developed, and lived out by the people who lead. If the people don't actually live out their stated values, then others will not buy into what they are being invited into.

When the Culture element of Momentum was developed, one of our major goals was to help you intentionally grow a healthy culture in your church. The two tools that we created for this element are the culture-carrier tool, which is designed to help staff culture get healthier, and the culture-shaper tool, which should help the overall culture improve.

Culture-carrier tool

This tool is designed to help you and your staff team live out your core values intentionally, together. Think about it. If you are claiming a set of core values as a church, but the people who lead are not intentionally living out those values, then eventually people will pick up on the lack of authenticity. The goal is for those who lead to live out the very values that they are inviting the church to live out. If the leaders live those values, it will cultivate an environment in which the culture can spread:

- Culture-carrier information: Every organization has a staff/leadership culture, whether they created one intentionally or it just happened. Make no mistake about it: we all have a leadership culture. The important thing for every organization is to be intentional in cultivating and growing the culture based on the leadership team they want. It is important for the culture to align with the organization's vision and values. The culture-carrier tool is designed to help your team cultivate an environment in which to build a team of staff members and key volunteer leaders who are culture carriers.

- Culture ambassador: The Momentum team believes it is important to assign a staff member to be culture ambassador. This is someone on the team who can devote a few hours each week to plan the culture-carrier environment. The ambassador can develop a team to help them, depending on the size of the staff team.

It is important to use the culture-carrier tool to think of ways to grow a healthy culture that is aligned with the vision and values of the church. The tool has weekly, monthly, quarterly, and bi-annual/annual activities, some of which are listed here:

- Retreats: Build trust, unity, and understanding
- Fun: Make it a place that works for their lives and families
- Rewards: What is rewarded is repeated
- Celebrate: Why it matters and how they made it work

Goals for a culture-carrier tool:

- Understand each other better
- Build trust
- Learn together
- Relax and have fun
- Increase understanding of the vision and values

Culture Carrier Tool

Weekly	Monthly
1.	1.
2.	2.
3.	3.
4.	4.
5.	5.
Quarterly	Bi-Annual/Annual
1.	1.
2.	2.
3.	3.
4.	4.

The Culture Carrier Tool is designed to help your staff team cultivate an environment to build a team of staff members and key lay leaders who are culture carriers.

Culture-shaper tool

This second tool in the Culture element aims to help your team grow a healthy culture around the core values of the church or organization. Used by your culture carriers, the tool will help them lead the organization to brainstorm and develop a strategy whereby people can experience the core values and vision of the church in a multisensory way. The tool follows a process to creatively deliver the core values.

The culture-shaper tool is designed to help each church determine how its values will be infused into the lives of the existing members, and new people, who collectively make up the church. We believe this is achieved by the way leaders lead and live their lives. Culture can be increased by creatively infusing the environment through a multisensory approach, which is why we created the culture-shaper tool.

A multisensory approach is important because we all experience the world through our senses, so you want to allow people to experience your church through their senses.

The tool has the five senses listed, and you will ask your leadership team to help you use the tool to determine creative ways to communicate the church's values through the multisensory approach. It is valuable to have all your staff fill out the tool. This will allow them to share their ideas and will help you to gather the best ideas across your whole organization.

Culture Shaper Tool

See	Hear
1.	1.
2.	2.
3.	3.
4.	4.
5.	5.
Touch	Smell
1.	1.
2.	2.
3.	3.
4.	4.

Taste	
1.	3.
2.	4.

The question to ask regarding each sense is how you can creatively use all the senses to help people learn and experience the values of your church. I should point out that many of the examples and ideas that your team will come up with will impact more than just one of the senses. People experience culture through their senses, and it can be powerful when they experience a life-giving culture.

Examples of culture-shape-tool ideas:

- First-time guest gift/t-shifts
- Second-time guest gift box/gift
- Notes to volunteers from staff celebrating them living out a value
- Quarterly volunteer party nights
- Branding volunteers: change-makers, dream team, etc.
- VIP volunteer lounge
- Change-maker minute (celebration of a volunteer each week)
- Love week (week-long local mission projects)
- Story videos around values
- Offering stories
- Pictures around your property
- Pictures with words around the property and online
- Sticky statements displayed around the property and online
- Visual pathway with values
- Value statements displayed
- Quality coffee and refreshments
- Social media stories/images
- Weekend team weekly huddle stories/values

- Property and facilities communicating values
- Follow-up document process communicating values
- Give follow-up process communicating values
- Smells in bathrooms, kids' area, lobby, auditorium
- Printed materials communicating values
- Website communicating values
- Next step/membership classes/growth track to teach values
- After-worship-service party (welcome event after services)
- Sermon series annually around values
- Guest-service teams knowing values
- Pre-service video showing values lived out

The culture-shape and culture-carrier tools can be extremely helpful in building and growing a healthy culture. To do so, you must be willing to utilize both tools to work on the culture.

↗RECAP

As stated in this chapter multiple times, culture is everything. If your culture is off, then your plans will be doomed to fail. The culture element of Momentum, and each of the tools within the Momentum model, is intended to help you grow a healthier culture in your church.

The culture-carrier tool is designed to help each of your leaders become carriers of the culture so the vision can be fulfilled. The culture-shaper tool is designed to creatively communicate your core values so people can experience them. We believe this will accelerate buy-in from people and make your culture contagious and healthier. These tools take a lot of work, but the pay-off is worth the time invested.

In the following chapter you will learn about the Measures element of Momentum.

CHAPTER 5

Measures

Crossroads Church had been struggling for several years, and the pastor had been trying to figure out how to experience numerical growth again. It had been over ten years since the church had seen growth, but the pastor believed the church could turn things around. Each week the church counted the people who came on a Sunday and the offering taken each week, and these two measures taken together was the church's metric for measuring its effectiveness.

The pastor knew that success was not based solely on how many people came each week or how much those people gave financially. The problem was his staff team and all the people in the church were basing their success solely on attendance and finances. As the church struggled, the pastor began to feel stressed. He felt that he had to keep the people happy. If they saw any further decline, the church might have to lay off staff or even close down.

This pressure was heavy on the pastor and the staff team, so much so that over a decade of trying to keep everyone happy the church had created a culture of dependency. This culture kept every staff member running in every direction, trying to ensure that all the church members remained happy.

The staff team had created an expectation among the church members that a pastor or staff member would always be available. People began to expect a staff member at their children's school event, at the hospital if a family member was sick, or at any gathering of a Bible study group, and the list goes on.

This culture of dependency was wearing down the staff. Their spouses were frustrated and their own children were neglected because of their demanding schedules. The church staff had become a group that was expected to be at everything and to be there for everyone all the time. It was an unhealthy culture. This culture of dependency and expectation had created a situation that was very challenging. Even if they had wanted to grow, there was not enough time because the church staff was consumed with meeting the members' unrealistic expectations.

The pastor wanted to see the church grow, but he knew that if he tried certain things he could be fired. He couldn't put his family through the loss of his job. He was also concerned that if he were fired, some of the other staff might also get fired. And he was also worried that even it he didn't get fired, some of the members would get upset because their needs were not being met. They might leave the church and they could not afford to lose anyone financially.

The pressure of all these potential things happening negatively affected the pastor's vision and creativity, and his willingness to take a risk.

The story of Crossroads Church is a common reality for many pastors and their church staff teams. They want to grow and would love to see something great happen, but the fear of all the things listed above keep them stuck. In this scenario the staff gets trapped into giving their time and energy to things that are not the most important.

Every pastor that deals with the realities in this story asks the same question: how do we change our situation? The culture described in the story is not one that can be changed quickly, but it is important to begin taking steps to shift from a culture of dependency to one of empowerment. The staff team must shift from the position of ministering to the people to a new position of equipping the people who are members to minster to others.

Momentum has two tools in the element we call Measures. The first is the dashboard tool, and the second is the good-vs.-great-organization tool.

Dashboard tool

This tool is a simple process where you refer back to the Big-Picture Process element. We encourage you to look at your purpose statement, core values, and long-range goals. These three things will help your team determine what should be the metrics that make up your dashboard. This tool and process will help your church measure what matters based on what you say is most important to the church leadership (purpose and core values). Having a dashboard that measures what really matters will help you determine your effectiveness beyond simply attendance and financials.

To be clear, I still encourage the measuring of attendance and finances, but also ensure that you measure other things that align with your vision, purpose, and values. As Peter Drucker said: "What gets measured gets done."

Each church staff team has to determine what matters to them: what they value, and how and what they measure. Your measures need to be driven by your values and your goals as a church. The goals that you set should be driven by your dreams and goals that are set by using the Big-Picture Process element.

To give you a jumpstart, after the next paragraph is a list of multiple examples of things many churches measure.

This is an important document to include as part of your weekly 100-minute meeting; it is part of that process. Whatever you decide to put on the dashboard, it is very important for the team to know what the wins are for the organization. As you redefine these wins, you can change the conversation about what is success. This gives you the opportunity to celebrate multiple things in your different environments and communication outlets.

For each area you measure, it is important for your team to set the number or percentage that you believe is challenging for your team. Measurement questions:

- Weekend attendance
- Monthly engagement
- Financials
- Salvations
- Baptisms
- First-time guests
- Second-time guests
- Membership class attendance
- Percentage of average attendance in small groups
- Percentage of people involved in mission work

Good-vs.-great-organization tool

This is the second tool in the Measures element of
Momentum that can help shift the culture from dependency
to empowerment. It's a simple tool that is designed to help
your team take the church's calendar, and everything that
is being done by the employees, and start eliminating or
delegating things. This tool should also be used with the
vision, purpose, and core values in mind as you use it to
filter the calendar and responsibilities.

There are two versions of this tool, but they are
used in the same way. Working together, the team will
use the organization version to list the organization's
responsibilities, and items on the calendar, and put them
in one of the four quadrants:

1. Top-right quadrant: high impact/high return = great
   results
2. Top-left quadrant: high impact/low return = good
   results
3. Bottom-right quadrant: low impact/high return = good
   results
4. Bottom-left quadrant: low impact/low return = bad
   results

When you have made this evaluation, you are ready to move onto the next step:

- Bad results: Items that fall in the bottom-left quadrant should be placed on a list to be stopped immediately, or a plan needs to be put in place to remove the items from the church's calendar or responsibilities.
- Good results: Items that fall in the top-left or bottom-right quadrant need to be reviewed, and the team needs to determine how to delegate or give less of their time to the less productive items.
- Great results: Items that fall in the top-right quadrant indicate a need for the team to give them more time and attention. These are the items that give the greatest results and have the greatest impact and return. It is important to make this more of the team's focus.

Organization

Good vs. Great Tool

High Impact

<table>
<tr>
<td rowspan="2">Low
Return</td>
<td></td>
<td></td>
<td rowspan="2">High
Return</td>
</tr>
<tr>
<td></td>
<td></td>
</tr>
</table>

Low Impact

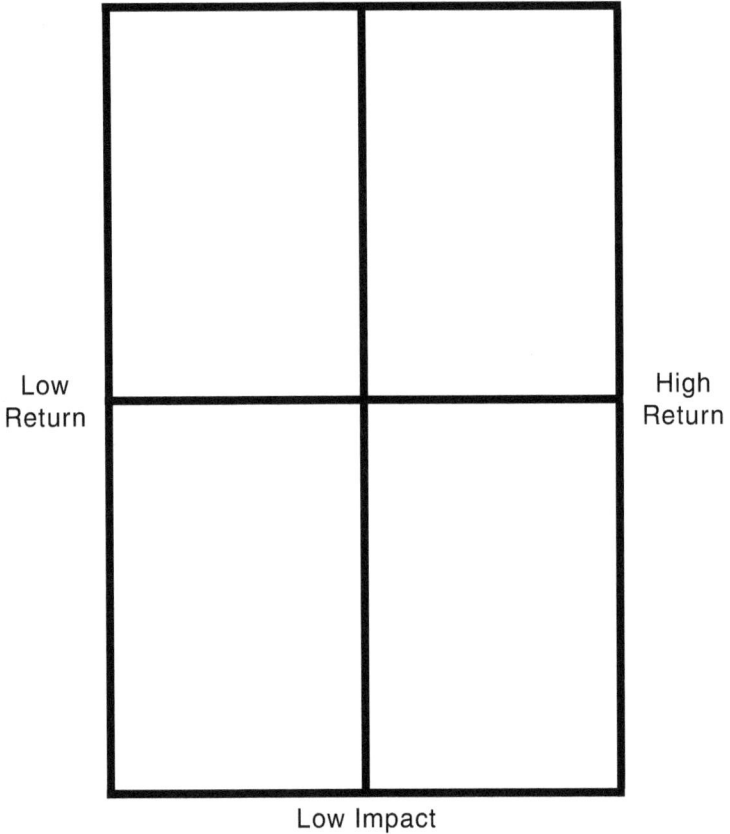

After your team uses this tool, the goal is for your church to stop doing some of the less productive things it has been doing. Also, delegate some of the things the staff has been doing to teams or members within the church. This is a very important step; it is crucial to move from a dependency culture to an empowerment one.

It is important to take care not to delegate without equipping. This shift can be a hard one for staff teams to make because they might think it is easier to do it themselves. This mentality might make things easier in the short term, but it will hold you hostage and keep you from unlocking the potential within your church for exponential growth. It will also build a culture within your staff team where they are not overworking.

The book of Ephesians teaches the church pastors to be the equippers, not the doers. If your church is going to have growth and health, it must equip and empower people to lead and do the work of ministry. "Now these are the gifts Christ gave to the church: the apostles, the prophets, the evangelists, and the pastors and teachers. Their responsibility is to equip God's people to do his work and build up the church, the body of Christ." (Ephesians 4:11-12)

↗RECAP

The Measures element of Momentum is probably the most simplistic, but it is still very important. The dashboard tool is really just a process to challenge you and your team to look back at the big-picture tool that you worked through earlier and make sure that you are measuring the things that you claim matter to you (this is a part of the weekly 100-minute meeting that you will learn about in the following chapter).

The good-vs.-great-organization tool in the Measures element is about helping your organization as a whole to focus on doing the most important things. I have always told the teams I have led that I would rather do less with excellence than do too much that is average. Make sure to use this tool and take action, because the less you do, the more effective you can be at what you do.

In the final chapter you will discover the Momentum element, and how the 100-minute-meeting tool works to help you gain momentum.

CHAPTER 6

Momentum

One of the most common conversations I have had in my years of leadership has been about meetings. It is almost funny to say that one of the key tools to making the Momentum process work is a meeting, but it is true. Effective meetings can transform the way trust is built, information is communicated, and clear plans are made. I have worked in organizations that had strong meeting structures that were very helpful. On the other hand, I have worked and led in organizations where the meetings were awful and we paid for it. I learned this the hard way when I first became a senior pastor. The way I led meetings was boring, unproductive, and unclear.

The frustrating thing to me was that I knew the meetings were boring and unproductive, but I didn't know exactly how to change it. This frustration is what led to the development of the 100-minute-meeting tool. I was blessed to experience a few good meeting structures, and the difference between them and the unproductive meetings I had been in, and even led, was drastic.

I had experiences through a friend who taught me new ways to lead meetings that helped me reshape the structure. I knew, after all the unproductive meetings I had sat through and led, that I wanted to revamp the meeting process I used.

The same friend also influenced the books I read. The two books that really helped me were *Traction* by Geno Wickman and *Death by Meeting* by Pat Lencioni. The big takeaways I took from both books was that our meetings needed to be engaging, focused, and productive.

When you use the 100-minute-meeting tool explained in this chapter on the Momentum element, you will discover that it creates an engaging environment that is focused and very productive. It is the secret sauce behind gaining momentum and keeping it. The 100-minute meeting is a game-changer when it comes to getting things done and transforming the way your church operates. At first the idea of a 100-minute meeting might seem a little overwhelming and long, but let me assure you that the time goes by fast. Also, when you implement this in the operations of your church, it will forever change how you get things done.

The 100-minute meeting is designed to drive the Big-Picture Process that the senior-level staff team has used to lay out the long-range plans for the church. That senior-level team gets together for planning every three months and revisits the big-picture-tool document they created. Each time they meet, they create ITAs (items to accomplish) for the next three months based on the long-range plan. This process keeps the team focused on the plan and moves the church forward in the plan. The team also creates additional ITAs that they need to accomplish for their individual areas of responsibility.

100-minute-meeting tool

As part of the discussion about this tool, we start with a basic agenda:

Team prayer	10 minutes
Celebrate	10 minutes
Dashboard	5 minutes
Review ITAs (items to accomplish)	5 minutes
Review last week's to-do list	5 minutes
The NDA list (name it, drill down, act on it)	60 minutes
Close meeting (read over to-do list, pass it on, pray)	5 minutes

71

The agenda explained:

- Team prayer: We believe that prayer is the most important factor for health and growth. This is why we suggest beginning each meeting with an intentional time of prayer. The team prayer time can be practiced however you like, but your challenge is to have some intentional time of prayer for each other, and for the church community. *(Ten minutes)*
- Celebrate: The time of celebration is a very important aspect, when the team members quickly share one thing they want to thank God for within the church body and one personal thing they are thankful to the Lord for. It will help you keep up with what is going on with each of your team members to hear what they are celebrating within the church and also personally. *(Ten minutes)*
- Dashboard: The third component of the 100-minute meeting is to read out loud the measures from the dashboard that the team has determined are the most important things to track. This is not a time to discuss the reasons why the goal the team is measuring has or has not been achieved. Instead, it is a time to simply verbalize if the measures were or were not met.

If something is being measured in the dashboard that is consistently coming up short, or is way off the mark and there is concern, it needs to be put on the NDA list (explained below). This can also be a time to add to the NDA list any goal that is being exceeded and needs more discussion or celebration. *(Five minutes; read the measures now and discuss them in detail later in the meeting)*

- Review ITAs list: The ITAs are determined for the overall church each quarter when the senior-level leadership team of the church has their three-month meeting. These are the major items that the church wants to accomplish over the next three months that are aligned with the five-, three- and one-year dreams of the church.

  To be clear, there are two lists of ITAs: the first list is the overall church ITAs for the next three months, and the second list is the individual ITAs for the next three months. A designated team member reads both lists of ITAs out loud each week during the 100-minute meeting. This is done to make sure that everyone knows the status of each ITA. If there is an ITA that is not on track to be completed by the set date, it needs to be moved to the NDA list. *(Five minutes; the discussion of one of the ITAs happens during the time allotted for the NDA-list)*

- Read last week's to-do list: Each week the team designates a team member to read the previous week's to-do list. When the list is read out loud for each individual team member, that person says "done" or "not done." If there is something on their list that is not done that item needs to be added to the NDA list, so that team member can update the team on why it didn't get done.

This might sound like a tough process, and it can be. But it will accelerate things and make sure they get done. Of course there are times when things are "not done" and the team member is able to share, during the NDA-list time, what is going on, so you need to be gracious to your teammates. As this process is adopted and practiced throughout the organization, it will create a culture where things get done. It is guaranteed to increase productivity and keep things from falling through the cracks. *(Five minutes; a critically important part of the 100-minute meeting)*

- The NDA list: NDA stands for *name* it, *drill* it, and *act* on it. This process takes up the bulk of the time in the 100-minute meeting and can last up to sixty minutes, but is incredible if done consistently and correctly. Each week during your weekly 100-minute meeting you will list the different issues, obstacles, and challenges that have come out of what is going on in the church. This list is compiled from things going on in the church, the ITA quarterly list that needs more discussion, and items on the past week's to-do list that were not done. This will give your leadership team a chance to get to the root of problems by naming them, drilling down, and acting with a solution.

Each item or obstacle is named and placed on the NDA list. Then the leadership team drills down to get to the root cause of the listed item. This gives the team clarity; they know what action needs to be taken because they have a clear next step for the relevant team member or members. They will then be able to act on it and get the item removed from the list.

It is critical that each item on the list has a clear action that is assigned to a specific person who will responsible. These actions will be read out loud the following week in the next 100-minute meeting.

This portion of the meeting needs to be led by someone on the team who can really help the team drill down on the items listed and get to the root of any obstacle. That person needs to be able to help identify the next step, and ensure that there is a clear to-do for someone on the team. On occasion, there will not be a to-do from an item discussed, but the majority of the time there will be. *(Sixty minutes)*

- Close meeting: The last portion of the meeting is made up of three quick steps. The first is to read out loud the to-do list that was just made during the NDA process. The second step is to list anything that needs to be passed onto the rest of the staff team members from the meeting. The third and final step is to close the time together with pray for the Lord to bless the plans that were made in the meeting and anything else the team wants to offer in prayer. *(Five minutes)*

↗RECAP

The final element is called Momentum because it will enable you to gain the momentum you are looking for if you implement the 100-minute-meeting tool. This tool in this element is key for executing the overall Momentum model. It truly is the glue that holds the whole process together. As you begin the process of implementing Momentum, I am confident you will see incredible results.

CONCLUSION

Our goal is that every leader or pastor who incorporates the Momentum model into their organization will follow the instructions given in this book. If you choose to self-implement the process, be aware that it will take about six months before you find a rhythm and feel like you are gaining the momentum you are hoping to gain. We do recommend that for the best results you contact us and allow us to help you implement the process. We believe this will result in the best results for your church or organization. Please let us know how we can help you on your journey.

ABOUT THE AUTHOR

Dr. Eric Smith is founder of Momentum. He has been married to Krystal for 14 years and they have a son, Weathers. Eric holds a Masters of Divinity and Doctorate of Ministry from Liberty University.

Eric brings 17 years of leadership experience, with 10 of those years spent as a senior pastor. His senior leadership includes being the co-founder of Vertical Church, a church plant in Mississippi that became one of the fastest growing churches in the state and grew to include four campuses. During that same time period, Eric co-founded the 242 Network, a church-planting network that assesses, trains and coaches church planters.

After almost 7 of leadership as a church planter and 242 Network director, Eric took on the task of revitalizing

Vaughn Forest Church in Montgomery, Alabama, a church that had been declining for almost 8 consecutive years. Under Eric's leadership, the church saw the momentum change and within a year and a half, Vaughn Forest Church was named in *Outreach Magazine*'s list of 100 Fastest Growing Churches in America, being ranked the 55th fastest growing church in America.